# Vital Signs Monitoring of Wolf (*Canis lupus*) Distribution and Abundance in Denali National Park and Preserve, Central Alaska Network

*2011 Report*

Natural Data Series NPS/CAKN/NRDS—2011/204

Thomas Meier
National Park Service
Denali National Park and Preserve
P.O. Box 9
Denali Park, AK  99755

November 2011

U.S. Department of the Interior
National Park Service
Natural Resource Stewardship and Science
 Fort Collins, Colorado

The National Park Service, Natural Resource Stewardship and Science office in Fort Collins, Colorado publishes a range of reports that address natural resource topics of interest and applicability to a broad audience in the National Park Service and others in natural resource management, including scientists, conservation and environmental constituencies, and the public.

The Natural Resource Data Series is intended for timely release of basic data sets and data summaries. Care has been taken to assure accuracy of raw data values, but a thorough analysis and interpretation of the data has not been completed. Consequently, the initial analyses of data in this report are provisional and subject to change.

All manuscripts in the series receive the appropriate level of peer review to ensure that the information is scientifically credible, technically accurate, appropriately written for the intended audience, and designed and published in a professional manner.

This report received informal peer review by subject-matter experts who were not directly involved in the collection, analysis, or reporting of the data. Data in this report were collected and analyzed using methods based on established, peer-reviewed protocols and were analyzed and interpreted within the guidelines of the protocols.

Views, statements, findings, conclusions, recommendations, and data in this report do not necessarily reflect views and policies of the National Park Service, U.S. Department of the Interior. Mention of trade names or commercial products does not constitute endorsement or recommendation for use by the U.S. Government.

This report is available from Center for Resources, Science and Learning, Denali National Park and Preserve and the Natural Resource Publications Management website (http://www.nature.nps.gov/publications/nrpm/).

Please cite this publication as:

NPS 965/111508, November 2011

# Contents

                                                                                      Page

Executive Summary ............................................................................................ v

Acknowledgments ............................................................................................. vi

Introduction ...................................................................................................... 1

Measurable Objectives ...................................................................................... 1

Methods and Materials ...................................................................................... 2

Results and Discussion ..................................................................................... 2

    Captures and Radio Telemetry ..................................................................... 2

    Wolf Pack Sizes and Density Estimates ....................................................... 3

    Mortality ...................................................................................................... 4

Plans for the Coming Year ................................................................................ 4

Literature Cited ................................................................................................. 5

Appendix A  Tables and Figures ....................................................................... 7

    Table 1.  Early-winter (fall) density of wolves, Denali National Park and
    Preserve, 1986-2010. ................................................................................... 8

    Table 2.  Late-winter (spring) density of wolves, Denali National Park and
    Preserve, 1986-2011. ................................................................................... 9

    Table 3.  Wolf pack sizes, Denali National Park and Preserve, 2007-2011. ......... 10

    Figure 1.  Wolf pack territories and population estimate for Denali National Park
    and Preserve, 2005. ..................................................................................... 15

    Figure 2. Wolf pack territories and population estimate for Denali National Park
    and Preserve, 2006. ..................................................................................... 16

    Figure 3. Wolf pack territories and population estimate for Denali National Park
    and Preserve, 2007 ...................................................................................... 17

    Figure 4. Wolf pack territories and population estimate for Denali National Park
    and Preserve, 2008. ..................................................................................... 18

# Contents (continued)

Page

Figure 5. Wolf pack territories and population estimate for Denali National Park and Preserve, 2009..................................................................................................... 19

Figure 6. Wolf pack territories and population estimate for Denali National Park and Preserve, 2010..................................................................................................... 20

Figure 7. Wolf pack territories and population estimate for Denali National Park and Preserve, 2011..................................................................................................... 21

Figure 8.  Wolf density estimates, Denali National Park and Preserve, 1986-2011.............. 22

Figure 9.  Wolf density estimates, Denali National Park and Preserve, 1986-2011,............. 23

spring and fall estimates on the same plot. .......................................................................... 23

Figure 10.  Locations of  VHF- and GPS-collared wolves, 1986-2011. .............................. 24

Figure 11.  Denali National Park and Preserve, showing areas of differing wolf management. ........................................................................................................................ 25

# Executive Summary

Wolves have been monitored with the use of radio collars in Denali National Park and Preserve since 1986. This work was conducted by the National Park Service (NPS) from 1986 to 1994, by the U. S. Geological Survey (USGS) from 1995 to 2002, and again by NPS from 2003 to 2011. A total of 162 wolves have been captured since NPS resumed wolf monitoring efforts in 2003. Between February 2010 and March 2011, 24 wolves were captured and radio collared in or near the Park and Preserve.

Each year, 10 to 15 wolf packs are monitored in or adjacent to the Park and Preserve. A total of 42 different wolves have worn GPS collars which determine the animal's location with an onboard GPS system and upload the data through the ARGOS satellite system. Of 97 collared wolves that died between 2003 and 2011, 40 were killed by humans and 57 by natural causes, suggesting an increase in human-caused mortality in recent years. The estimate of wolf density in March 2011 was 4.0 wolves per 1000 square kilometers, slightly higher than the density a year earlier but still lower than the long-term average of 5.4 wolves per 1000 square kilometers.

The elimination of the Stampede and Nenana Canyon Closed Areas, which formerly protected wolves in certain areas adjacent to Denali, along with the presence of intensive management and predator control programs adjacent to the Park and Preserve, has prompted concerns about impacts to the natural and healthy status of Denali's wolf populations, and impacts to visitor opportunities for viewing wolves in the Park. A new study, conducted by Bridget Borg of the University of Alaska and the National Park Service, will use specially designed GPS collars to study the movements of wolves living adjacent to the park road, and will analyze wolf movements and wolf mortality patterns to address these questions.

# Acknowledgments

John Burch and Bridget Borg (NPS) captured wolves and provided suggestions for data analysis. Helicopter pilots Rick Swisher (Quicksilver Air) and Troy Cambier (Chena River Aviation), and fixed-wing pilots Dennis Miller (Caribou Air), Sandy Hamilton (Arctic Air Alaska), and Colin Milone (National Park Service) piloted aircraft on wolf capture and radio-tracking flights. Melanie Cook of the National Park Service, Dr. Sandy Talbot of the U. S. Geological Survey, and Dr. Robert Wayne of the University of California, Los Angeles,  performed genetic analysis of wolf specimens.  Dr. Edward DeBevec of the University of Alaska, Fairbanks, developed an online tool for decoding and managing wolf location data obtained from GPS/ARGOS telemetry collars.  Telonics, Inc. (Mesa, AZ) developed radio collar designs to address unique problems of monitoring wolves in Alaska.  Dr. Kimberlee Beckman of the Alaska Department of Fish and Game performed wolf necropsies and arranged for immunological testing of wolf blood specimens.  The Washington Animal Disease Diagnostic Laboratory performed immunological testing of wolf specimens.  Jane Bryant, Denise Albert, N. J. Gates, Tyler Danielson, Bridget Borg, and Melissa Snover served as observers during wolf capture operations.  Philip Hooge, John Burch and Maggie MacCluskie (NPS) reviewed this manuscript and provided additions and corrections.

# Introduction

This report summarizes efforts to monitor wolves (*Canis lupus*) in Denali National Park and Preserve (DENA), Alaska, through spring 2011. Wolves occur in all three parks of the Central Alaska Monitoring Network (CAKN): Denali National Park and Preserve, Yukon-Charley Rivers National Preserve, and Wrangell-St. Elias National Park and Preserve. Wolves are one of six keystone large mammal species in interior Alaska, along with grizzly bears (*Ursus arctos*), black bears (*Ursus americanus*), moose (*Alces alces*). caribou (*Rangifer tarandus*), and Dall's sheep (*Ovis dalli*). Wolves are of great importance to people from both consumptive and non-consumptive viewpoints, and to the ecosystem as a whole. As a top predator, wolves may play a key role in influencing ungulate populations, and as a result may influence vegetation patterns (Miller et al. 2001, Ripple and Beschta 2003). The effects of wolves on ungulate populations (Mech and Peterson 2003) may be important determinants of ungulate availability for subsistence harvest on NPS Park and Preserve lands in Alaska, and harvest by the general public on NPS Preserve lands (National Park Service 2003). Data obtained from wolf monitoring are used to assist with wolf den site protection and other aspects of the Denali Wolf-Human Conflict Management Plan (National Park Service 2007).

Wolves are a species specifically identified in the enabling legislation and management objectives of all three CAKN parks (U. S. Congress 1980). Wolves are of great importance to park visitors because of the unique opportunities to view wolves in Alaskan parks. While the primary objective of monitoring is to track the distribution and abundance of wolves, a variety of additional data is obtained in the monitoring process. This information is likely to have great value for wildlife management and research. The body of data on wolf populations in Alaska parks is of great value in developing scientific models of predator/prey systems. In heavily visited portions of the parks, managers want to know the locations of active wolf dens and rendezvous sites (pup rearing areas) so that they can be protected from disturbance. When intensive wolf harvest or wolf control take place near parks, it is vital to know the patterns of travel of park packs, in order to determine whether they are being significantly impacted by activities outside of the parks. Data on the genetic, morphological, and immunological characteristics of wolves, obtained in the course of wolf capture, will be important in evaluating long-term changes in wolf populations in Alaska.

Parkwide monitoring of wolves in Denali National Park and Preserve was initiated by Resource Management Ranger John Dalle-Molle in 1986, with principal investigators L. David Mech and Layne Adams. Field work between 1986 and 1994 was performed by John Burch and Tom Meier. From 1995 through 2002, Layne Adams, now with USGS, conducted wolf monitoring efforts. Since 2003, John Burch and Tom Meier have again conducted the field work.

# Measurable Objectives

- Locate non-radiocollared wolf packs using Park and Preserve lands by snow tracking.
- Capture and radio-collar 1-3 individuals in each wolf pack identified in the study area.
- Determine the demography (numbers, colors, age structure) of monitored wolf packs.
- Obtain morphological measurements from captured wolves.

- Obtain genotypic data (mitochondrial and microsatellite DNA) from captured wolves.
- Obtain immunological (disease exposure) data from captured wolves.
- Determine pack size for each collared pack in fall (early winter) and spring (late winter).
- Define the mosaic of wolf home ranges (population area) for estimating wolf densities.
- Perform annual capture efforts to maintain coverage of radio collars in the population.
- Detect pack extinction and pack formation events in the population.
- Detect changes in wolf density over time.
- Detect changes in wolf pack sizes over time.
- Detect changes in wolf home ranges over time.
- Detect changes in the morphological, immunological, and genetic makeup of the wolf population over time.
- Investigate the effects of wildlife management activities on the natural and healthy character of wolves in Denali.
- Investigate the biological and social characteristics of wolf viewing by visitors in Denali, and factors that may affect wolf viewing opportunities.

## Methods and Materials

Methods of wolf monitoring used in DENA followed the Wolf Monitoring Protocol for Denali National Park and Preserve, Yukon-Charley Rivers National Preserve and Wrangell-St. Elias National Park and Preserve, Alaska (Meier et al. 2009). An exception to this is the determination of wolf pack territories (Figures 1-7). Wolf pack territories were not rigorously calculated using the 95% of locations that would produce the smallest home range. An appropriate protocol (e.g. harmonic mean removal of dispersed points) must be developed in order to automate this task. The present wolf pack territories were produced by manually removing selected wolf locations that were thought by the author to represent extraterritorial forays or pre-dispersal movements by the collared animals.

## Results and Discussion

### Captures and Radio Telemetry

Five wolves from 4 packs were captured and radio-collared in winter 2009-2010, and 19 wolves from 9 packs were captured in winter 2010-2011 (Table 4). The Iron Creek Pack, occupying the mountain slope in the west end of the park, was first collared in February 2010. One new pair of wolves (The Alder Creek Pair) was discovered when an adult male wolf from the East Fork Pack paired with a wolf of unknown origin, but the male wolf was trapped and killed on the Toklat River shortly afterward. GPS-collared wolves from the Bearpaw and Somber Packs dispersed west to the North Fork and South Fork of the Kuskokwim River, respectively, and established packs there. The years 2010 and 2011 saw the extinction of several wolf packs that had previously been followed, including the Toklat Springs, Totek Hills, Chitsia, and Mount Margaret Packs in the northeastern part of the study area, and the Otter Lake and Tonzona Packs to the west. Collared wolves from the Kantishna River and Somber Packs began travelling together in winter 2010-2011, and these two packs appear to have merged.

Morphological data, including sex, weight, age and color, and blood and tissue samples for genetics and disease analysis, were gathered from captured wolves. Morphologic data is presented in Table 4. Genetics results are being analyzed by biologists at the United States Geological Survey Alaska Science Center (USGS) and University of California Los Angeles (UCLA). Wolves living in or near Denali have been occasionally been found to be infested with the dog louse *Trichodectes canis* and also with another coat abnormality of unknown origin (Beckmen et al. 2009, Wolstad et al. 2009). Immunological surveys of wolves in interior Alaska have revealed exposure to a number of diseases but have not detected evidence of serious population effects of disease (Mech et al. 1998, Zarnke and Ballard 1987). One disease that has the potential to seriously affect wolf pup survival is Canine Parvovirus (CPV). Immunological studies of Denali wolves have revealed a rate of exposure to CPV as high as 50% in some years, among wolves that were captured and blood sampled (R. Zarnke, pers. comm.).

Between May 1, 2009 and April 30, 2011, collared wolves were located approximately twice per month by aircraft. A total of 49 different radio-collared wolves from 23 packs were monitored for some or all of this period, resulting in 1,477 locations of collared wolves. In addition, 3,709 locations were obtained from 20 wolves that wore GPS/ARGOS collars for some or all of this period. The Telonics GPS collars used on most of these wolves obtain one location each day and store the location coordinates within the collar. The data is uploaded weekly through the ARGOS satellite system, and also remains stored within the collar so that all data can be uploaded when the collar is retrieved. In March 2011, six specially designed GPS collars were placed on wolves that live near the park road; two each from the East Fork, Grant Creek, and McKinley Slough Pack. Designed to provide more detailed data on the movements of these packs, the collars determine each wolf's location every 3 hours. The road study GPS collars are equipped with breakaway devices and will fall from the wolves in September 2012. Further information on this study can be found below. Since 2003, more than 15,900 wolf locations have been obtained from GPS/ARGOS collars. Since 1986, more than 15,600 wolf locations have been obtained by conventional radio telemetry. The locations of all collared wolves in this study's 25-year history are plotted in Figure 8 in the Appendix.

## Wolf Pack Sizes and Density Estimates

Aircraft surveys in spring 2011 observed 71 wolves, 21 of them radio-collared. These wolves were found in 10 packs covering an area of 117,994 square kilometers, mostly within the boundaries of Denali National Park and Preserve north of the Alaska Range (Figure 7 and Table 3, in Appendix). This produced a density estimate of 3.94 wolves per 1000 square kilometers, a slight increase from the spring 2010 count of 59 wolves in 12 packs and density of 3.46 wolves per 1000 square kilometers. Wolf densities for the past 3 years have been the lowest in Denali since 1987 (Table 1 and 2, Figures 8 and 9). No obvious explanation for this low density is apparent, and wolf numbers may have begun to rebound.

The present method of determining wolf density involves the use of minimum convex polygons to estimate individual wolf pack territories, and combining a number of territories into a larger, non-convex polygon representing the population. In implementing this method, subjective decisions are by made NPS wildlife biologists to exclude forays by wolf packs outside of their usual range, so that the population area is not inflated by the inclusion of areas that are actually occupied by other, uncollared wolf packs. CAKN personnel are developing methods using kernel estimators (White and Garrott 1990) that might provide a more objective estimate of pack territory sizes and wolf densities (J. Burch and J. Schmidt, pers. comm). Dispersing or lone wolves were not included in population size or density estimates.

### Mortality

Sixteen radio-collared wolves died between 1 May 2009 and 30 April 2011. Seven were legally shot, trapped or snared outside of the Park/Preserve. Nine died of natural causes. Table 4 (see Appendix) summarizes the fates of wolves captured and radio-collared between March 2003 and March 2011. Of 87 radio-collared wolves that were captured during this period and subsequently died, at least 34 (39%) were killed by humans. Two of those were trapped within Park/Preserve boundaries by qualified subsistence users, and the remainder were killed outside of Park/Preserve boundaries. The data suggest an increase in human-caused mortality in the Denali wolf population. During the period 1986-1994, only 8 (14%) of 58 mortalities of radio-collared wolves were human-caused (Mech et al. 1998).

Beginning in 2000, the State of Alaska established the Stampede Closed area to protect wolves west of the Savage River (Figure 11) from harvest, in order to preserve wolf viewing opportunities in Denali National Park. In 2003, the Nenana Canyon Closed Area, a narrow strip of land east of the George Parks Highway, was created for the same purpose. In March 2010, the Alaska Board of Game voted to eliminate both of these closed areas. No radio-collared wolves were killed by humans during winter 2010-2011, in these areas newly opened to wolf harvest.

Intraspecific strife (the killing of wolves by members of neighboring wolf packs) probably remains the leading cause of wolf mortality in DENA (Mech et al. 1998), but many carcasses are consumed or decomposed before they can be investigated, so that only 39% of natural mortality between 2003 and 2011 was documented as wolf-caused, while most mortalities were classified as of unknown natural cause. It is likely that many of these mortalities were also wolf-caused.

## Plans for the Coming Year

In 2011-2012, we plan to maintain contact with approximately 10-12 wolf packs inside or partly inside Denali National Park and Preserve. Collars will be maintained on 2 members of each pack if possible, with additional collars on the East Fork, Grant Creek, and McKinley Slough Packs as part of a two-year study of wolf movements, wolf viewing, and wolf mortality by University of Alaska Fairbanks graduate student and park employee Bridget Borg. Monitoring efforts will continue, with wolves being located about twice per month, with extra monitoring flights in spring and fall to document pack sizes and pup production.

# Literature Cited

Beckmen, K.B., G.D. Bossart, and K. Burek. 2009. A novel dermatopathy in Alaskan gray wolves (*Canis lupus*). Poster presentation at the Northwest Sectional Meeting of the Wildlife Society, Fairbanks, AK.

Mech, L. D., L. G. Adams. T. J. Meier, J. W. Burch, and B. W. Dale. 1998. The Wolves of Denali. University of Minnesota Press, MN. 227 pages.

Mech, L. D., and R. O. Peterson. 2003. Wolf-prey relations. Pp. 131-160 *In* Mech, L.D., and L. Boitani, eds., Wolves: Behavior, Ecology, and Conservation. University of Chicago Press, IL. 448 pp.

Meier, T. J., 2009. Vital signs monitoring of wolf (*Canis lupus*) distribution and abundance in Denali National Park and Preserve, Central Alaska Network. 2009 report. Natural Resource Data Series NPS/CAKN /NRDS 2009/009. National Park Service, Fort Collins, Colorado.

Meier, T. J., Burch, J. W., Wilder, D., Cook, M. 2009. Wolf monitoring protocol for Denali National Park and Preserve, Yukon-Charley Rivers National Preserve and Wrangell-St. Elias National Park and Preserve, Alaska. Natural Resource Report PS/CAKN/NRRR—2009/168. National Park Service, Fort Collins, CO.

Miller, B., B. Dugelby, D. Foreman, C. Martinez del Rio, R. Noss, M. Phillips, R. Reading, M. E. Soule', J. Terborgh, and L. Willcox. 2001. The importance of large carnivores to healthy ecosystems. Endangered Species Update 18: 202-210.

National Park Service, 2003. Subsistence management plan, Denali National Park and Preserve.

National Park Service, 2007. Wolf-human conflict management plan, Denali National Park and Preserve. Denali National Park and Preserve, AK. 85 pp.

National Park Service, 2010. Are wolf viewing opportunities at risk? Fact sheet. National Park Service, Denali Park, AK 99755 2 pp. http://www.nps.gov/dena/naturescience/upload/wolfbuffer2010.pdf

Ripple, W.J., and R. L. Beschta. 2003. Wolf reintroduction, predation risk, and cottonwood recovery in Yellowstone National park. Forest Ecology and Management 184: 299-313.

U. S. Congress. 1980. Alaska National Interest Lands Conservation Act, PUBLIC LAW 96-487-DEC. 2, 1980. 94 STAT. 2371. http://www.r7.fws.gov/asm/anilca/toc.html

White, G. C., and R. A. Garrott. 1990. Analysis of wildlife radio-tracking data. Academic Press, San Diego, CA.

Wolstad, T., K. Beckmen, C. Gardner, F. Huettmann, and K. Hundertmark. 2009. Lousy wolves: Distribution and habitat assessment of Trichodectes canis, an invasive ectoparasite of Alaskan gray wolves. Poster presented at the Northwest Section meeting of The Wildlife Society, Fairbanks, AK.

Zarnke, R.L., and W.B. Ballard. 1987. Serological survey for selected microbial pathogens of wolves in Alaska, 1975-1982. J. Wildl. Dis. 23:77-85.

Zarnke, R.L., J. Evermann, J.M. VerHoef, M.E. McNay, R.D. Boertje, C.L. Gardner, L.G. Adams, B.W. Dale, and J.W. Burch. 2001. Serologic survey for canine coronavirus in wolves from Alaska. J. Wildl. Dis. 37:740-745.

# Appendix A  Tables and Figures

**Tables**

Table 1.  Early-winter density of wolves, Denali National Park and Preserve, 1986-2010.

Table 2.  Late-winter density of wolves, Denali National Park and Preserve, 1986-2011.

Table 3.  Wolf pack sizes, Denali National Park and Preserve, 2004-2011.

Table 4.  Wolf captures, Denali National Park and Preserve, 2003-2011.

**Figures**

Figure 1.  Wolf pack territories and population estimate for Denali National Park and Preserve, 2005.

Figure 2. Wolf pack territories and population estimate for Denali National Park and Preserve, 2006.

Figure 3. Wolf pack territories and population estimate for Denali National Park and Preserve, 2007.

Figure 4. Wolf pack territories and population estimate for Denali National Park and Preserve, 2008.

Figure 5. Wolf pack territories and population estimate for Denali National Park and Preserve, 2009.

Figure 6. Wolf pack territories and population estimate for Denali National Park and Preserve, 2010.

Figure 7. Wolf pack territories and population estimate for Denali National Park and Preserve, 2011.

Figure 8.  Wolf density estimates, Denali National Park and Preserve, 1986-2009.

Figure 9.  Wolf density estimates, Denali National Park and Preserve, 1986-2009, spring and fall estimates on the same plot.

Figure 10.  Locations of VHF- and GPS-collared wolves, 1986-2009.

Figure 11. Map of Denali National Park and Preserve showing zones of wolf management.

Table 1. Early-winter (fall) density of wolves, Denali National Park and Preserve, 1986-2010.

| YEAR | NUMBER OF PACKS MONITORED | TOTAL WOLVES IN PACKS MONITORED | COMBINED AREA OF MONITORED PACKS (KM$^2$) | ESTIMATED DENSITY: WOLVES / 1000 KM$^2$ | POPULATION ESTIMATE INSIDE THE PARK* |
|---|---|---|---|---|---|
| 1986 | 4 | 22 | 8,180 | 2.7 | 46 |
| 1987 | 9 | 70 | 13,150 | 5.3 | 92 |
| 1988 | 14 | 121 | 14,670 | 8.2 | 142 |
| 1989 | 11 | 127 | 15,240 | 8.3 | 144 |
| 1990 | 11 | 136 | 13,930 | 9.8 | 169 |
| 1991 | 13 | 137 | 14,275 | 9.6 | 166 |
| 1992 | 15 | 120 | 13,620 | 8.8 | 152 |
| 1993 | 12 | 93 | 9,900 | 9.4 | 162 |
| 1994 | 12 | 72 | 11,145 | 6.5 | 112 |
| 1995 | 11 | 80 | 12,045 | 6.6 | 115 |
| 1996 | 11 | 104 | 12,776 | 8.1 | 141 |
| 1997 | 12 | 75 | 12,808 | 5.9 | 101 |
| 1998 | 12 | 68 | 12,578 | 5.4 | 93 |
| 1999 | 15 | 80 | 12,699 | 6.3 | 109 |
| 2000 | 18 | 112 | 14,554 | 7.7 | 133 |
| 2001 | 18 | 91 | 13,802 | 6.6 | 114 |
| 2002 | 14 | 86 | 12,226 | 7.0 | 121 |
| 2003 | 11 | 84 | 11,682 | 7.2 | 124 |
| 2004 | 14 | 78 | 14,630 | 5.3 | 92 |
| 2005 | 15 | 106 | 15,367 | 6.9 | 119 |
| 2006 | 17 | 111 | 17,439 | 6.4 | 110 |
| 2007 | 20 | 147 | 17,757 | 8.3 | 143 |
| 2008 | 14 | 86 | 16,607 | 5.2 | 89 |
| 2009 | 15 | 89 | 17,061 | 5.2 | 90 |
| 2010 | 11 | 88 | 17,994 | 4.9 | 84 |

* wolf estimate = the calculated wolf density projected across an estimated 17,270 square km of potential habitat within park boundaries, north of the Alaska Range

Table 2.  Late-winter (spring) density of wolves, Denali National Park and Preserve, 1986-2011.

| YEAR | NUMBER OF PACKS MONITORED | TOTAL WOLVES IN PACKS MONITORED | COMBINED AREA OF MONITORED PACKS (KM$^2$) | ESTIMATED DENSITY: WOLVES / 1000 KM$^2$ | POPULATION ESTIMATE INSIDE THE PARK |
|---|---|---|---|---|---|
| 1986 | 4 | 26 | 7,380 | 3.5 | 61 |
| 1987 | 8 | 37 | 12,125 | 3.1 | 53 |
| 1988 | 14 | 69 | 15,355 | 4.5 | 78 |
| 1989 | 13 | 98 | 16,810 | 5.8 | 101 |
| 1990 | 10 | 106 | 13,930 | 7.6 | 131 |
| 1991 | 13 | 111 | 14,275 | 7.8 | 134 |
| 1992 | 15 | 103 | 13,620 | 7.6 | 131 |
| 1993 | 12 | 68 | 9,900 | 6.9 | 119 |
| 1994 | 10 | 61 | 11,145 | 5.5 | 95 |
| 1995 | 12 | 59 | 12,120 | 4.9 | 84 |
| 1996 | 11 | 69 | 12,640 | 5.5 | 94 |
| 1997 | 11 | 78 | 13,080 | 6.0 | 103 |
| 1998 | 12 | 61 | 13,121 | 4.6 | 80 |
| 1999 | 13 | 69 | 12,699 | 5.4 | 94 |
| 2000 | 17 | 71 | 14,378 | 4.9 | 85 |
| 2001 | 16 | 87 | 13,802 | 6.3 | 109 |
| 2002 | 15 | 73 | 13,026 | 5.6 | 97 |
| 2003 | 18 | 75 | 11,682 | 6.4 | 111 |
| 2004 | 14 | 78 | 16,061 | 4.9 | 84 |
| 2005 | 15 | 66 | 14,630 | 4.5 | 78 |
| 2006 | 15 | 103 | 15,367 | 6.7 | 116 |
| 2007 | 16 | 93 | 17,439 | 5.3 | 92 |
| 2008 | 20 | 99 | 17,757 | 5.6 | 96 |
| 2009 | 16 | 65 | 16,607 | 3.9 | 68 |
| 2010 | 12 | 59 | 17,061 | 3.5 | 60 |
| 2011 | 10 | 71 | 17,994 | 3.9 | 68 |

*  wolf estimate = the calculated wolf density projected across an estimated 17,270 square km of potential habitat within park boundaries, north of the Alaska Range

Table 3.  Wolf pack sizes, Denali National Park and Preserve, 2007-2011.

| PACK | 2007 | | 2008 | | 2009 | | 2010 | | 2011 |
|---|---|---|---|---|---|---|---|---|---|
| | spring | fall | spring | fall | spring | fall | spring | fall | spring |
| ALDER CREEK | | | | | | | | | 1 |
| BEARPAW | 8 | 10 | 9 | 5 | 5 | 2 | 2 | 6 | 5 |
| BOOT LAKE | | 1 | (2) | 2 | 4 | 3 | (3) | (8) | (9) |
| CASTLE ROCKS | 5 | 7 | 7 | 2 | 0 | | | | |
| CHITSIA | 9 | 11 | 5 | 7 | 1 | 0 | | | |
| EAST FORK | 15 | 15 | 11 | 16 | 11 | 12 | 5 | 11 | 6 |
| GRANT CREEK | 5 | 5 | 3 | 6 | 6 | 14 | 11 | 16 | 16 |
| HAUKE | 4 | 4 | 3 | 0 | | | | | |
| HOT SLOUGH | 2 | 7 | 7 | 8 | 6 | 7 | 5 | 3 | 4 |
| IRON CREEK | | | | | 2 | 6 | 5 | 9 | 7 |
| KANTISHNA RIVER | 1 | 1 | 2 | 5 | 2 | 6 | 6 | 8 | 0 |
| MCKINLEY RIVER | 5 | 10 | 2 | 0 | | | | | |
| MCKINLEY SLOUGH | 8 | 15 | 15 | 14 | 11 | 15 | 14 | 19 | 18 |
| MCLEOD 2 | 4 | 6 | 2 | 0 | | | | | |
| MOOSE CREEK | | | | | 2 | 2 | 2 | 0 | |
| MT MARGARET | 6 | 7 | 3 | 2 | 2 | 5 | 0 | 0 | |
| NENANA RIVER | | | | | 2 | 6 | 2 | 5 | 4 |
| OTTER LAKE | | | | | 2 | 2 | 2 | 3 | 0 |
| PINTO | 3 | 10 | 4 | 0 | | | | | |
| SAVAGE | | 2 | 2 | 6 | 0 | | | | |
| SOMBER | 6 | 11 | 8 | 8 | 4 | 2 | 2 | 6 | 7 |
| STARR LAKE | 3 | 6 | 4 | 3 | 3 | 6 | 3 | 3 | 3 |
| TOKLAT SPRINGS | 6 | 9 | 6 | (5) | (1) | (3) | (3) | (3) | 0 |
| TONZONA | | (1) | (2) | 2 | 2 | 1 | 0 | 0 | |
| TOTEK HILLS | | 6 | 6 | (4) | (3) | 0 | 0 | 0 | 0 |
| TURTLE HILL | 3 | 4 | 0 | | | | | | |
| | | | | | | | | | |
| TOTAL WOLVES | 93 | 147 | 99 | 86 | 65 | 89 | 59 | 89 | 71 |
| AREA IN KM² | 17,439 | 17,757 | 17,757 | 16,607 | 16,607 | 17,061 | 17,061 | 17,994 | 17,994 |
| WOLVES/1000 KM² | 5.33 | 8.28 | 5.58 | 5.18 | 3.91 | 5.22 | 3.46 | 4.95 | 3.95 |
| EST WOLVES IN PARK* | 92 | 143 | 96 | 89 | 68 | 90 | 60 | 85 | 68 |

*  wolf estimate = the calculated wolf density projected across an estimated 17,270 square km of potential habitat within park boundaries, north of the Alaska Range

Peripheral packs, with sizes in parentheses, were not included in the density estimate that year.

Table 4.  Wolf captures, Denali National Park and Preserve, 2003-2011.

| WOLF | DATE | RECAP | SEX | AGE | COLOR | PACK | STATUS / FATE |
|------|------|-------|-----|-----|-------|------|---------------|
| 0087 | 03/16/03 | Yes | F | Adult ~8 | Dark Gray | Kantishna River | Recaptured, recollared |
| 0316 | 03/16/03 | No | M | Adult ~4 | Gray | Castle Rocks 2 | Killed by wolves |
| 9755 | 03/16/03 | Yes | F | Adult ~6 | Light Gray | Pinto | Shot west of Healy |
| 9974 | 03/16/03 | Yes | M | Adult ~2 | Dark Gray | Death Valley | Died, unknown natural causes |
| 0092 | 03/17/03 | Yes | F | Adult ~5 | Gray | Mount Margaret | Killed by wolves |
| 0317 | 03/17/03 | No | F | Adult ~3 | Black | Castle Rocks 2 | Snared near Lake Minchumina |
| 0079 | 03/18/03 | Yes | M | Adult ~6 | Blue | Muddy River | Died, unknown natural causes |
| 0089 | 03/18/03 | Yes | M | Adult ~6 | Gray | McKinley Slough | Missing |
| 0104 | 10/26/03 | Yes | M | Adult ~4 | Gray | Mount Margaret | Snared west of Healy |
| 0318 | 10/26/03 | No | F | Adult ~4 | Gray | East Fork | Snared west of Healy |
| 0103 | 10/27/03 | Yes | F | Adult ~4 | Gray | Grant Creek | Collar failed |
| 0319 | 10/27/03 | No | M | Adult ~2 | Gray | Death Valley | Trapped west of Healy |
| 0320 | 10/28/03 | No | F | Yearling | Gray | McKinley Slough | Missing |
| 0321 | 10/28/03 | No | F | Adult ~4 | Gray | Straightaway | Starved |
| 0322 | 10/28/03 | No | F | Yearling | Black | Kantishna River | Missing |
| 0401 | 02/18/04 | No | F | Yearling | Gray | Muddy River | Shot west of Healy |
| 0402 | 02/18/04 | No | F | Adult ~5 | Blue | Chitsia | Recaptured, recollared |
| 0403 | 03/06/04 | No | F | Adult ~4 | Gray | Turtle Hill | Collar failed |
| 0102 | 03/07/04 | Yes | F | Adult ~6 | Light Gray | 100 Mile | Died, probably starved |
| 0404 | 03/07/04 | No | M | Adult ~5 | Light Gray | 100 Mile | Starved |
| 0405 | 03/07/04 | No | F | Yearling | Gray | 100 Mile | Died of unknown causes |
| 0406 | 03/07/04 | No | F | Adult ~5 | Gray | Herron | Collar chewed off |
| 0407 | 03/07/04 | No | M | Adult ~2 | Gray | Herron | Collar chewed off |
| 0408 | 03/08/04 | No | F | Yearling | Gray | Mount Margaret | Recaptured, recollared |
| 0409 | 03/08/04 | No | F | Adult ~4 | White | Toklat Springs | Recaptured, recollared |
| 0410 | 03/08/04 | No | M | Yearling | Gray | Toklat Springs | Shot on lower Toklat River |
| 0411 | 03/08/04 | No | F | Yearling | Gray | Chitsia | Recaptured, recollared |
| 0412 | 03/08/04 | No | F | Adult ~4 | Gray | McKinley River | Died, unknown natural causes |
| 0413 | 03/08/04 | No | M | Pup | Gray | Castle Rocks 2 | Died, unknown natural causes |
| 0087 | 03/09/04 | Yes | F | Adult ~9 | Blue | Kantishna River | Starved |
| 0414 | 03/09/04 | No | M | Adult ~4 | Black | Bearpaw | Recaptured, recollared |
| 0415 | 03/09/04 | No | F | Adult ~3 | Gray | Bearpaw | Recaptured, recollared |
| 0416 | 03/09/04 | No | F | Pup | Gray | Starr Lake | Missing |
| 0411 | 03/04/05 | Yes | F | Adult ~2 | Gray | Chitsia | Collar failed |
| 0414 | 03/04/05 | Yes | M | Adult ~5 | Black | Bearpaw | Recaptured, recollared |
| 0501 | 03/04/05 | No | M | Adult ~3 | Gray | Mount Margaret | Recaptured, recollared |
| 0502 | 03/04/05 | No | F | Yearling | Gray | Mount Margaret | Died, unknown natural causes |
| 0503 | 03/04/05 | No | M | Adult ~2 | Gray | Chitsia | Recaptured, recollared |
| 0504 | 03/04/05 | No | M | Adult ~8 | White | Toklat Springs | Shot on lower Toklat River |
| 0505 | 03/05/05 | No | M | Adult ~3 | Gray | McKinley River | Recaptured, recollared |
| 0101 | 03/06/05 | Yes | F | Adult ~6 | Gray | Kantishna River | Killed by wolves |
| 0107 | 03/06/05 | Yes | F | Adult ~6 | Gray | McKinley Slough | Killed by wolves |
| 0506 | 03/06/05 | No | M | Adult ~3 | Black | Lone (Hult Creek) | Starved |
| 0507 | 03/06/05 | No | M | Adult ~3 | Black | Kantishna River | Killed by wolves |
| 0508 | 03/07/05 | No | F | Adult ~4 | Gray | Turtle Hill | Killed by wolves |

Table 4.  (Continued).  Wolf captures, Denali National Park and Preserve, 2003-2011.

| WOLF | DATE | RECAP | SEX | AGE | COLOR | PACK | STATUS / FATE |
|------|------|-------|-----|-----|-------|------|---------------|
| 0408 | 02/01/06 | Yes | F | Adult ~3 | Gray | Mount Margaret | Died from blunt trauma |
| 0601 | 02/01/06 | No | M | Adult ~2 | Black | Turtle Hill | Trapped west of Healy |
| 0403 | 02/08/06 | Yes | F | Adult ~6 | Light Gray | Turtle Hill | Recaptured, recollared |
| 0602 | 02/09/06 | No | F | Yearling | Gray | Toklat Springs | Shot on lower Teklanika River |
| 0605 | 02/23/06 | No | F | Pup | Black | East Fork | Shot near Cantwell |
| 0606 | 02/23/06 | No | M | Adult ~3 | Gray | Pinto | Died of unknown causes |
| 0607 | 02/23/06 | No | F | Adult ~5 | Gray | Pinto | Shot west of Healy |
| 0103 | 02/24/06 | Yes | F | Adult ~6 | Gray | Grant Creek | Killed by wolves |
| 0215 | 02/24/06 | Yes | M | Adult ~6 | Gray | Grant Creek | Killed by wolves |
| 0214 | 02/28/06 | Yes | F | Adult ~7 | Blue | McKinley River | Killed by wolves |
| 0505 | 02/28/06 | Yes | M | Adult ~4 | Gray | McKinley River | Recaptured, recollared |
| 0608 | 02/28/06 | No | F | Adult ~4 | Silver | Starr Lake | Drowned |
| 0609 | 02/28/06 | No | F | Adult ~3 | Black | Starr Lake | Recaptured, recollared |
| 0610 | 03/01/06 | No | F | Adult ~4 | Gray | Somber | Recaptured, recollared |
| 0611 | 03/01/06 | No | F | Yearling | Gray | Somber-Tonzona | Still being monitored |
| 0612 | 03/01/06 | No | F | Adult ~4 | Gray | Castle Rocks 3 | Recaptured, recollared |
| 0613 | 03/01/06 | No | M | Adult ~3 | Blond | Castle Rocks 3 | Missing |
| 0614 | 03/01/06 | No | M | Yearling | Gray | Toklat Springs | Trapped south of Healy |
| 0615 | 03/11/06 | No | M | Adult ~7 | White | Straightaway | Killed by wolves |
| 0616 | 04/17/06 | No | M | Pup | Gray | Kantishna River | Trapped in Minto area |
| 0617 | 04/17/06 | No | M | Pup | Black | Kantishna River | Recaptured, recollared |
| 0618 | 04/17/06 | No | F | Adult ~2 | Gray | East Fork | Recaptured, recollared |
| 0503 | 12/11/06 | Yes | M | Adult ~4 | Gray | Chitsia | Recaptured, recollared |
| 0620 | 12/11/06 | No | F | Yearling | Gray | Chitsia | Trapped north of park boundary |
| 0621 | 12/11/06 | No | F | Yearling | Gray | Toklat Springs | Trapped west of Healy |
| 0622 | 12/11/06 | No | M | Yearling | Gray | Grant Creek | Snared east of park boundary |
| 0701 | 02/14/07 | No | M | Adult ~2 | Gray | McKinley Slough | Missing |
| 0702 | 02/14/07 | No | M | Adult ~3 | Gray | McKinley Slough | Recaptured, recollared |
| 0703 | 02/14/07 | No | F | Adult ~8 | White | Hauke | Killed by wolves |
| 0704 | 02/14/07 | No | M | Adult ~4 | Gray | Hauke | Recaptured, recollared |
| 0402 | 02/27/07 | Yes | F | Adult ~8 | Gray | Chitsia | Died, unknown natural causes |
| 0409 | 02/27/07 | Yes | F | Adult ~6 | White | Pinto | Trapped west of Healy |
| 0705 | 03/01/07 | No | F | Yearling | Light Gray | McLeod 2 | Killed by wolves |
| 0706 | 03/01/07 | No | F | Adult ~7 | Gray | McLeod 2 | Died, unknown natural causes |
| 0707 | 03/01/07 | No | F | Adult ~2 | Gray | Lone (Boot Lake) | Still being monitored |
| 0505 | 03/03/07 | Yes | M | Adult ~5 | Gray | McKinley River | Died ,unknown natural causes |
| 0708 | 03/03/07 | No | F | Pup | Gray | Somber | Recaptured, recollared |
| 0709 | 03/03/07 | No | F | Pup | Gray | Bearpaw | Collar found near Manley |
| 0710 | 03/04/07 | No | F | Pup | Gray | Somber | Shot west of park boundary |
| 0711 | 03/04/07 | No | M | Pup | Gray | Totek Hills | Shot near lower Teklanika River |
| 0712 | 03/28/07 | No | F | Yearling | Black | East Fork/Savage | Trapped south of Healy |
| 0713 | 03/28/07 | No | M | Pup | Gray | Totek Hills | Died, unknown natural causes |
| 0610 | 03/29/07 | Yes | F | Adult ~6 | Gray | Somber | Died, unknown natural causes |
| 0612 | 03/29/07 | Yes | F | Adult ~5 | Blue | Castle Rocks 3 | Died, unknown natural causes |
| 0714 | 03/29/07 | No | F | Adult ~2 | Gray | Hot Slough | Killed by wolves |

Table 4. (Continued). Wolf captures, Denali National Park and Preserve, 2003-2011.

| WOLF | DATE | RECAP | SEX | AGE | COLOR | PACK | STATUS / FATE |
|------|------|-------|-----|-----|-------|------|---------------|
| 0715 | 03/29/07 | No | M | Adult ~2 | Gray | Hot Slough | Died, unknown natural causes |
| 0716 | 03/29/07 | No | M | Adult ~5 | Black | Starr Lake | Died, unknown natural causes |
| 0403 | 11/27/07 | Yes | F | Adult ~8 | White | Turtle Hill | Died, unknown natural causes |
| 0702 | 11/27/07 | Yes | M | Adult ~4 | Gray | McKinley Slough | Recaptured, recollared |
| 0717 | 11/27/07 | No | M | Adult ~5 | Silver | East Fork | Recaptured, recollared |
| 0718 | 11/27/07 | No | F | Adult ~5 | Light Gray | McKinley Slough | Died, unknown natural causes |
| 0719 | 11/27/07 | No | F | Adult ~2 | Gray | Grant Creek | Still being monitored |
| 0720 | 11/28/07 | No | M | Adult ~3 | Gray | McLeod 2 | Trapped north of park boundary |
| 0721 | 11/28/07 | No | M | Yearling | Gray | Hauke | Dispersed north |
| 0722 | 11/28/07 | No | F | Adult ~3 | Black | Kantishna River | Missing |
| 0723 | 11/29/07 | No | M | Adult ~3 | Gray | Toklat Springs | Died, unknown causes |
| 0724 | 11/29/07 | No | F | Pup | Gray | Totek Hills | Trapped north of park boundary |
| 0414 | 03/02/08 | Yes | M | Adult ~8 | Silver | Bearpaw | Died, unknown natural causes |
| 0415 | 03/02/08 | Yes | F | Adult ~7 | Gray | Bearpaw | Still being monitored |
| 0618 | 03/02/08 | Yes | F | Adult ~4 | Gray | East Fork | Recaptured, recollared |
| 0801 | 03/02/08 | No | M | Adult ~2 | Gray | Kabena | Pack moved north out of area |
| 0704 | 03/03/08 | Yes | M | Adult ~5 | Gray | Hauke | Killed by wolves after capture |
| 0802 | 03/03/08 | No | M | Yearling | Gray | Castle Rocks 3 | Died, unknown natural causes |
| 0803 | 03/03/08 | No | F | Yearling | Gray | Unk/Fish Camp | Died, unknown natural causes |
| 0609 | 03/04/08 | Yes | F | Adult ~5 | Black | Starr Lake | Missing |
| 0804 | 03/04/08 | No | M | Adult ~2 | Gray | Starr Lake | Recaptured, recollared |
| 0805 | 03/04/08 | No | F | Pup | Gray | Hot Slough | Still being monitored |
| 0806 | 03/04/08 | No | M | Adult ~2 | Gray | Castle Rocks 3 | Dispersed, shot in wolf control |
| 0807 | 04/02/08 | No | M | Adult ~3 | Gray | Savage | Not collared, last seen 12/08 |
| 0501 | 11/01/08 | Yes | M | Adult ~2 | Gray | Mount Margaret | Trapped west of Healy |
| 0810 | 11/01/08 | No | F | Adult ~2 | Gray | Toklat Springs | Trapped north of park boundary |
| 0811 | 11/01/08 | No | M | Adult ~3 | Gray | Grant Creek | Still being monitored |
| 0812 | 11/01/08 | No | F | Adult ~5 | Light Gray | McKinley Slough | Still being monitored |
| 0813 | 11/01/08 | No | F | Adult ~7 | Black | Mount Margaret | Killed by wolves |
| 0814 | 11/02/08 | No | M | Adult ~7 | Dark Gray | Totek Hills | Dispersed North |
| 0815 | 11/02/08 | No | F | Yearling | Yellow gray | Hot Slough | Trapped south of Minchumina |
| 0816 | 11/02/08 | No | F | Adult ~3 | Gray | McKinley Slough | Melted ice, drowned at capture |
| 0817 | 11/03/08 | No | M | Yearling | Dark Gray | Somber | Died, unknown natural causes |
| 0818 | 11/03/08 | No | M | Adult ~4 | Gray | Tonzona | Shot on Tonzona River |
| 0819 | 11/04/08 | No | M | Adult ~4 | Gray | Chitsia | Died, unknown natural causes |
| 0617 | 02/21/09 | Yes | M | Adult ~3 | Black | Kantishna River | Recaptured, recollared |
| 0722 | 02/21/09 | Yes | F | Adult ~4 | Black | Kantishna River | Died, unknown natural causes |
| 0901 | 02/21/09 | No | F | Yearling | Gray | Hot Slough | Died, unknown natural causes |
| 0902 | 02/22/09 | No | M | Adult ~2 | Black | Bearpaw | Dispersed to N Fork Kuskokwim |
| 0903 | 02/22/09 | No | F | Yearling | Gray | Somber | Dispersed to S Fork Kuskokwim |
| 0904 | 02/22/09 | No | M | Adult ~2 | Gray | Boot Lake | Still being monitored |
| 0905 | 02/23/09 | No | F | Yearling | Gray | Nenana River | Still being monitored |
| 0906 | 02/23/09 | No | M | Adult ~3 | Black | Mount Margaret | Shot NE of Healy |
| 0907 | 02/23/09 | No | F | Adult ~2 | Blue | Otter Lake | Died, unknown natural causes |
| 0908 | 02/23/09 | No | F | Adult ~2 | Black | Otter Lake | Dispersed to Mucha Lake area |

Table 4. (Continued). Wolf captures, Denali National Park and Preserve, 2003-2011.

| WOLF | DATE | RECAP | SEX | AGE | COLOR | PACK | STATUS / FATE |
|------|------|-------|-----|-----|-------|------|---------------|
| 0909 | 02/23/09 | No | F | Adult ~2 | Gray | Moose Creek | Killed by wolves |
| 0910 | 02/23/09 | No | M | Adult ~2 | Gray | Moose Creek | Died, unknown natural causes |
| 0911 | 02/24/09 | No | M | Adult ~3 | Gray | Nenana River | Killed by wolves |
| 0702 | 02/19/10 | Yes | M | Adult ~6 | Gray | Mckinley Slough | Still being monitored |
| 0804 | 02/19/10 | Yes | M | Adult ~4 | Gray | Starr Lake | Snared near Kantishna River |
| 1001 | 02/19/10 | No | F | Pup | Gray | Iron Creek | Still being monitored |
| 1002 | 02/19/10 | No | F | Adult ~5 | Light Gray | Iron Creek | Died, unknown natural causes |
| 1003 | 02/19/10 | No | M | Adult ~4 | Gray | Otter Lake | Shot at Telida Village |
| 0618 | 11/27/10 | Yes | F | Adult ~7 | Gray | East Fork | Still being monitored |
| 0717 | 11/27/10 | Yes | M | Adult ~8 | Silver | East Fork | Snared on Toklat River |
| 1004 | 11/27/10 | No | M | Yearling | Gray | Grant Creek | Still being monitored |
| 1005 | 11/27/10 | No | M | Pup | Gray | Unknown | Trapped in Dry Creek |
| 1006 | 11/29/10 | No | F | Pup | Black | Bearpaw | Still being monitored |
| 1007 | 12/01/10 | No | M | Pup | Dark Gray | Nenana River | Died, unknown natural causes |
| 1008 | 12/01/10 | No | F | Yearling | Black | Hot Slough | Still being monitored |
| 1009 | 12/01/10 | No | M | Yearling | Gray | Iron Creek | Still being monitored |
| 1101 | 03/08/11 | No | F | Yearling | Light Gray | East Fork | Still being monitored |
| 1102 | 03/08/11 | No | M | Pup | Black | East Fork | Still being monitored |
| 0811 | 03/10/11 | Yes | M | Adult ~5 | Gray | Grant Creek | Still being monitored |
| 1103 | 03/10/11 | No | F | Yearling | Gray | Grant Creek | Still being monitored |
| 1105 | 03/10/11 | No | M | Yearling | Gray | Nenana River | Still being monitored |
| 0617 | 03/11/11 | Yes | M | Adult ~5 | Black | Somber | Still being monitored |
| 0708 | 03/11/11 | Yes | F | Adult ~4 | Gray | Somber | Still being monitored |
| 1106 | 03/11/11 | No | F | Yearling | Gray | Mckinley Slough | Still being monitored |
| 1107 | 03/11/11 | No | M | Pup | Gray | Mckinley Slough | Still being monitored |
| 1108 | 03/11/11 | No | M | Adult ~3 | Gray | Iron Creek | Still being monitored |
| 1109 | 03/11/11 | No | M | Adult ~2 | Black | Somber | Still being monitored |

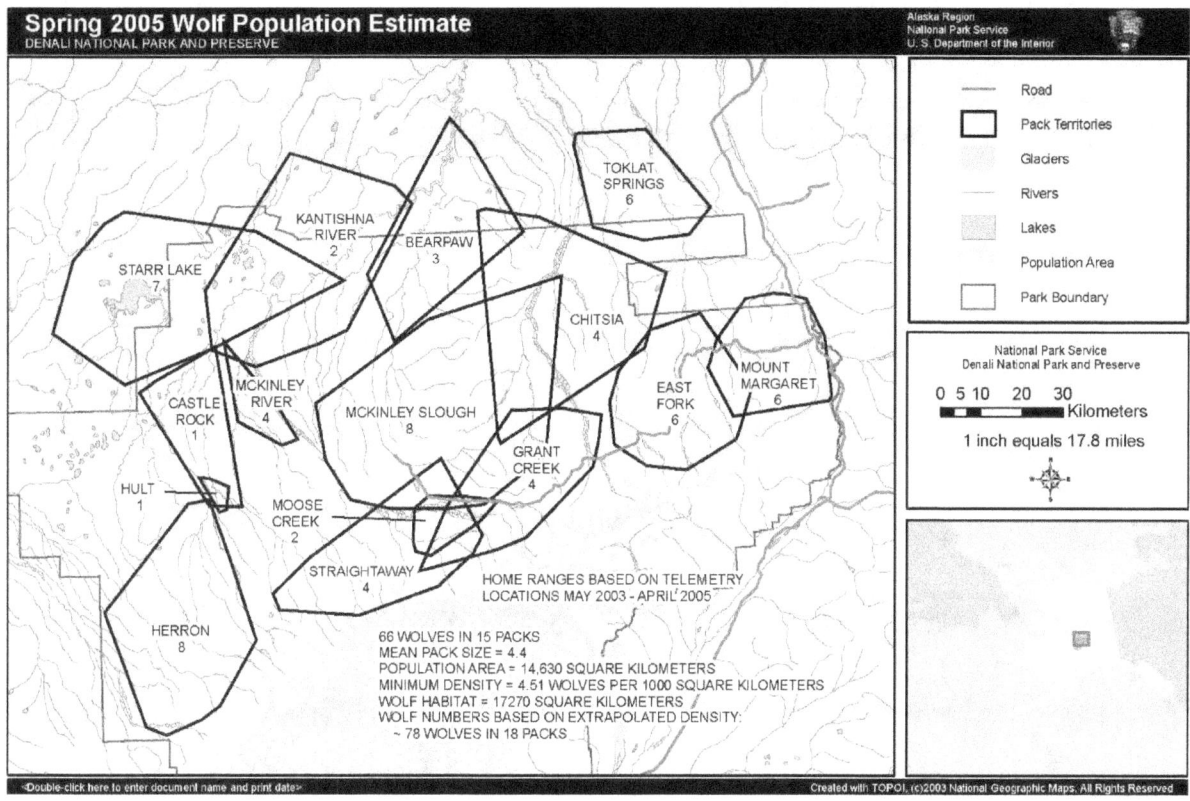

Figure 1.  Wolf pack territories and population estimate for Denali National Park and Preserve, 2005.

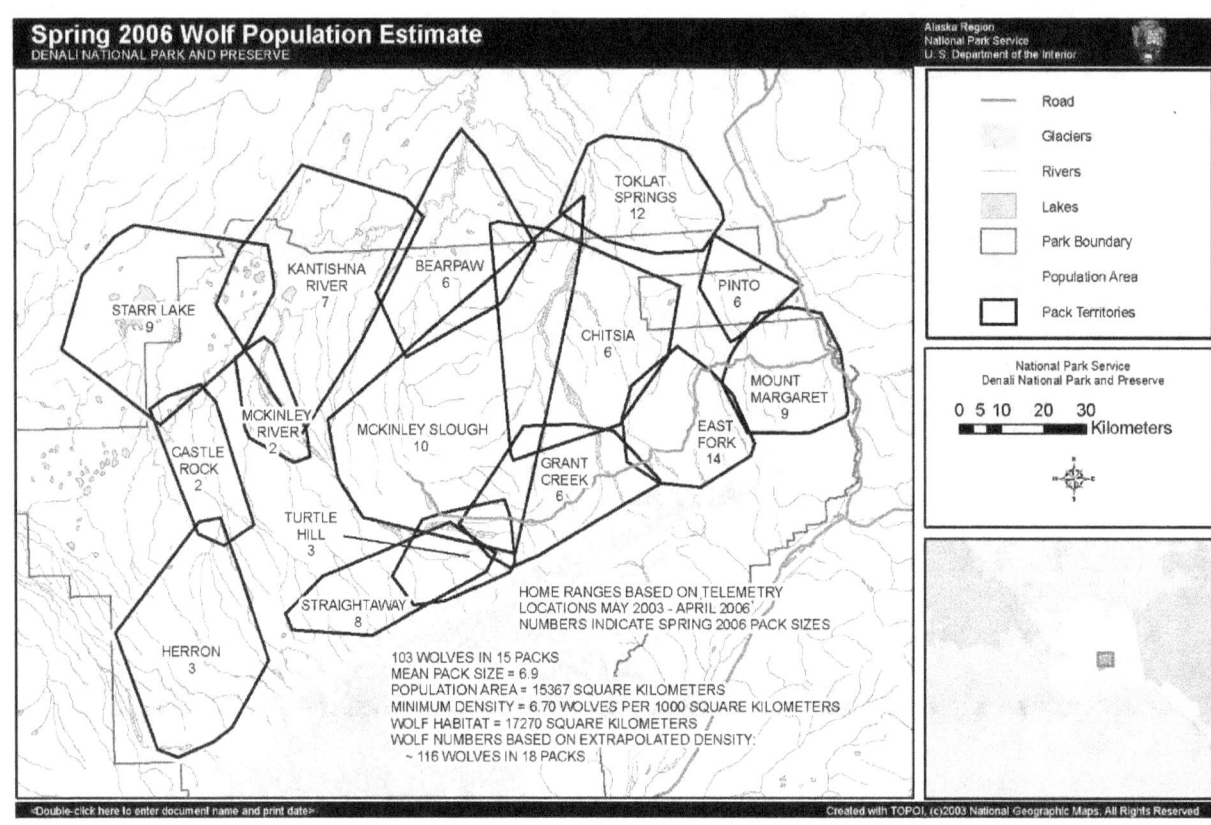

Figure 2. Wolf pack territories and population estimate for Denali National Park and Preserve, 2006.

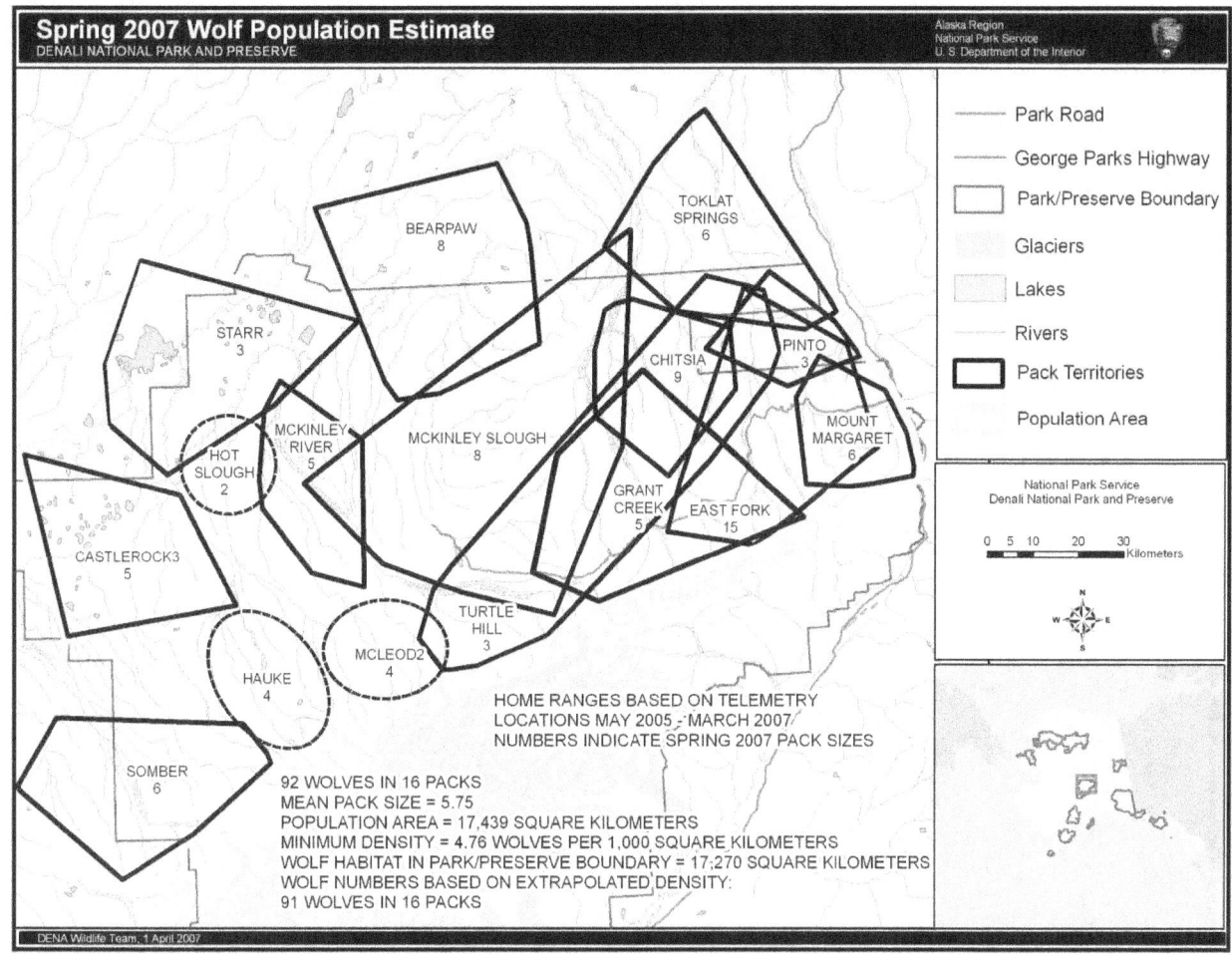

Figure 3. Wolf pack territories and population estimate for Denali National Park and Preserve, 2007

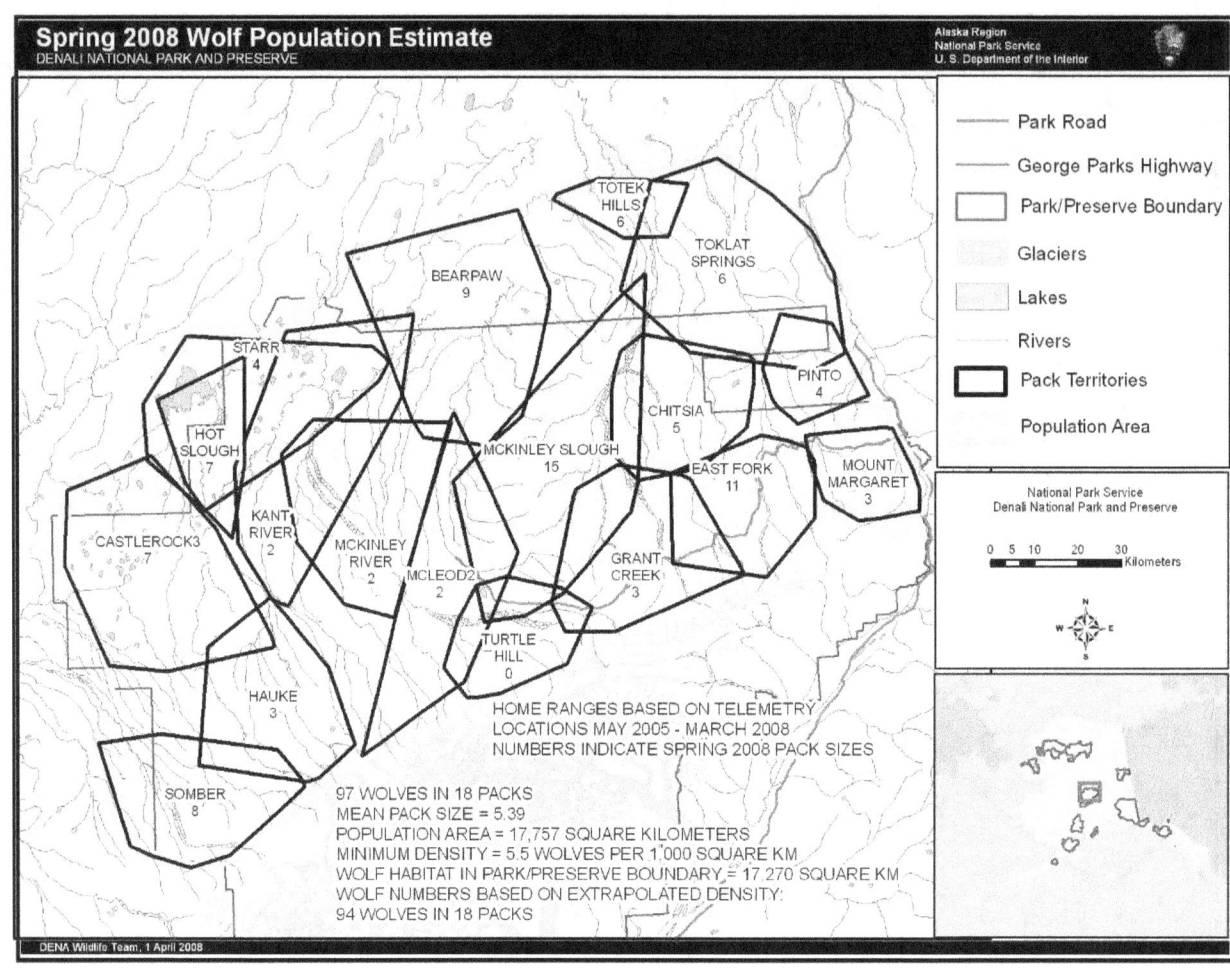

Figure 4. Wolf pack territories and population estimate for Denali National Park and Preserve, 2008.

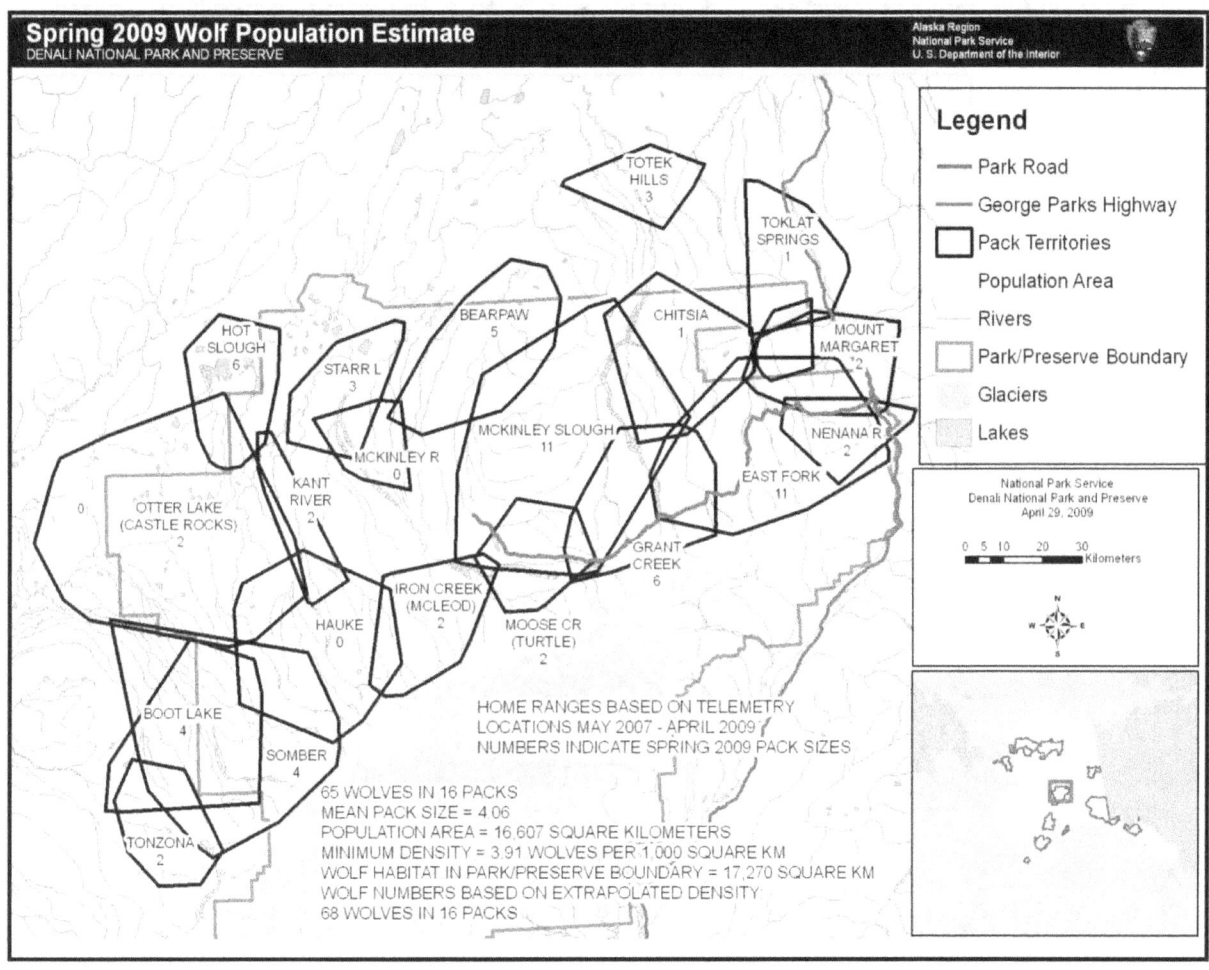

Figure 5. Wolf pack territories and population estimate for Denali National Park and Preserve, 2009.

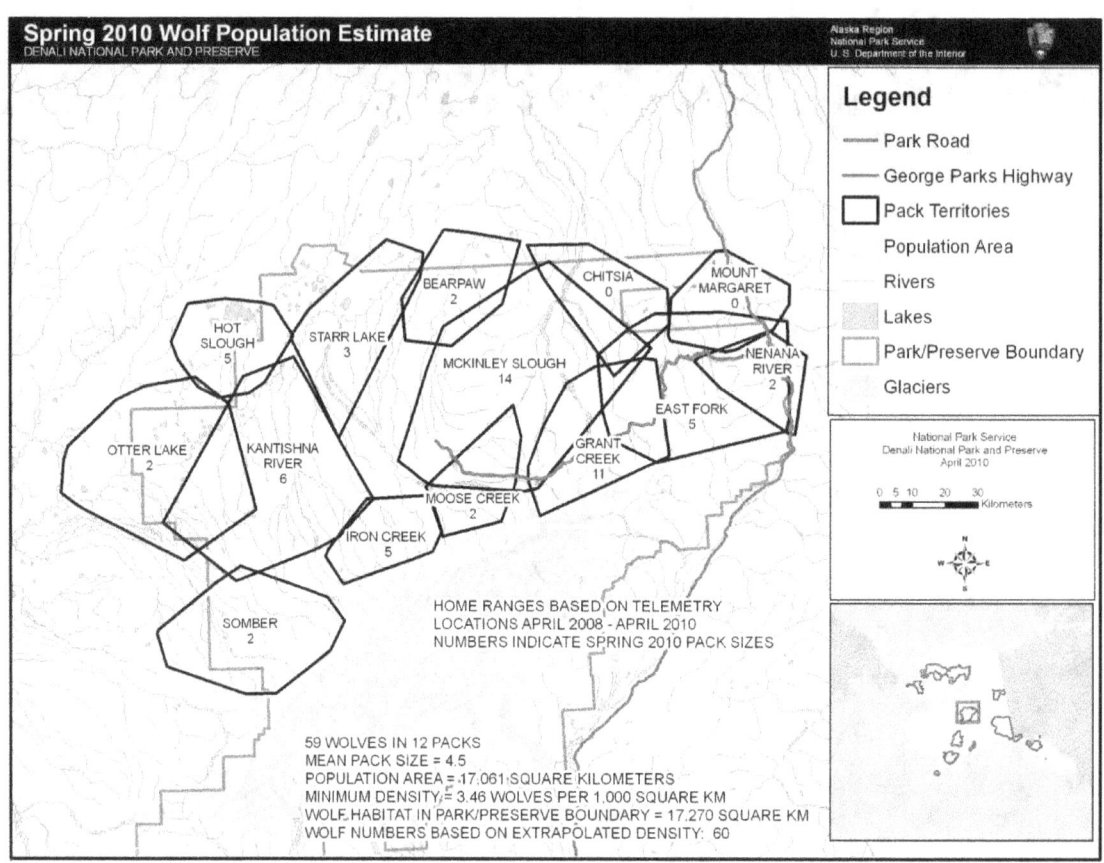

Figure 6. Wolf pack territories and population estimate for Denali National Park and Preserve, 2010.

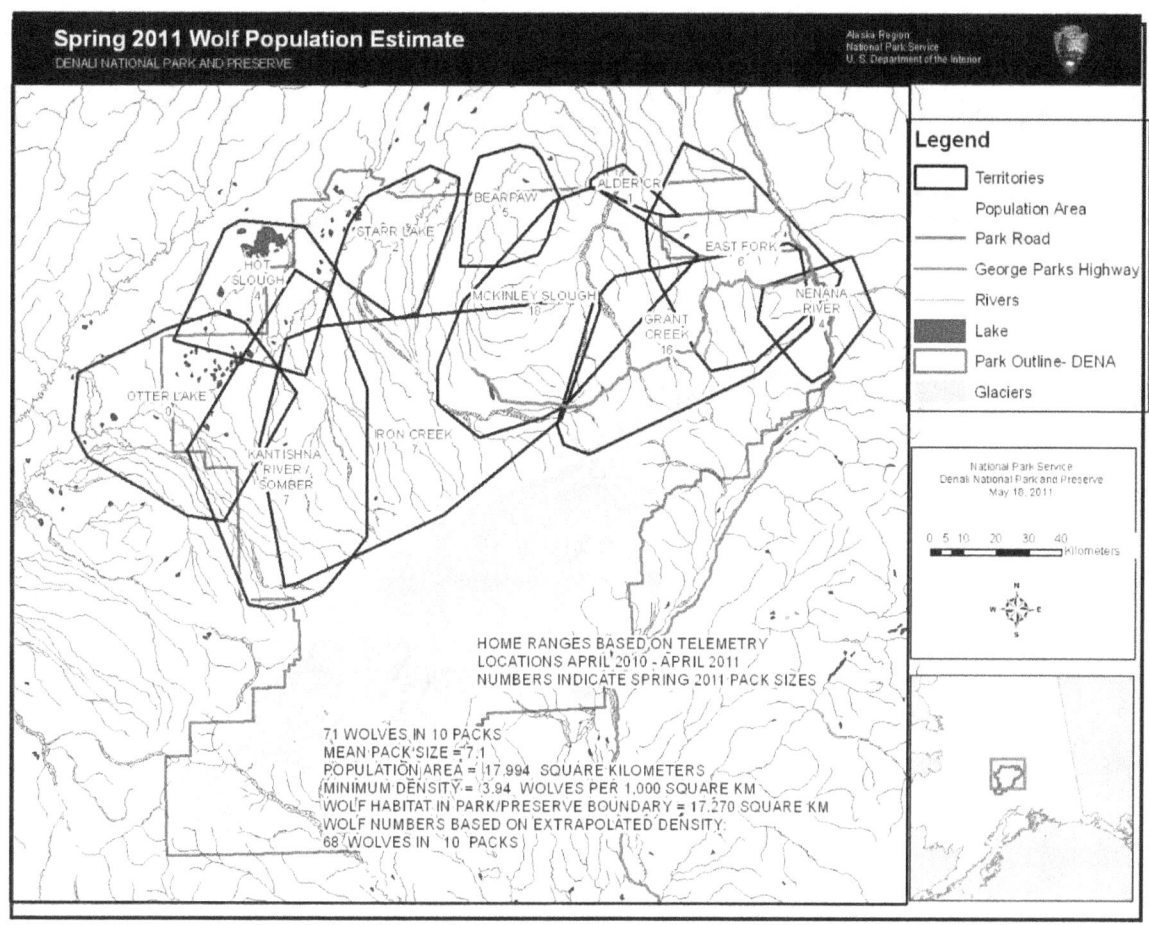

Figure 7. Wolf pack territories and population estimate for Denali National Park and Preserve, 2011.

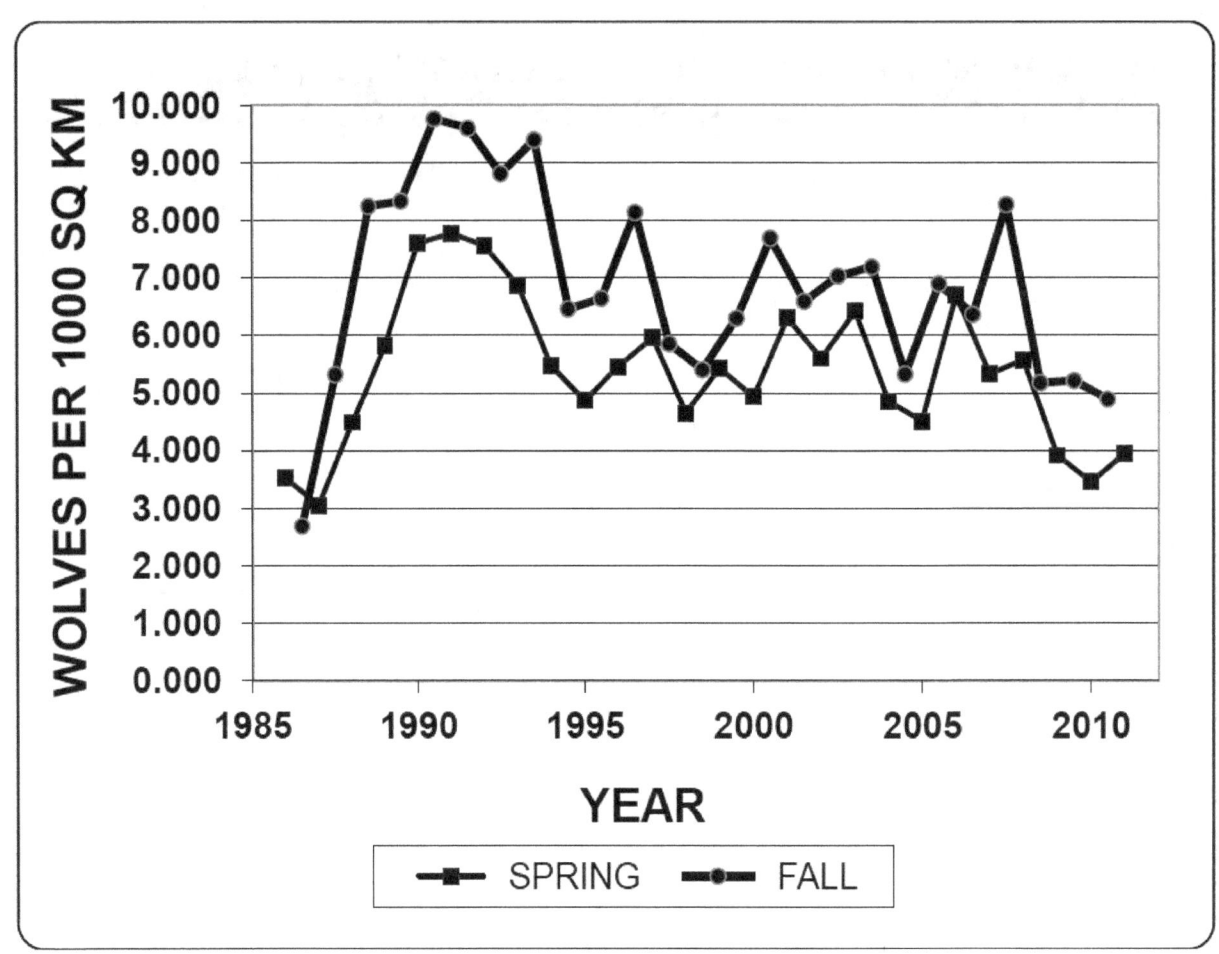

Figure 8. Wolf density estimates, Denali National Park and Preserve, 1986-2011.

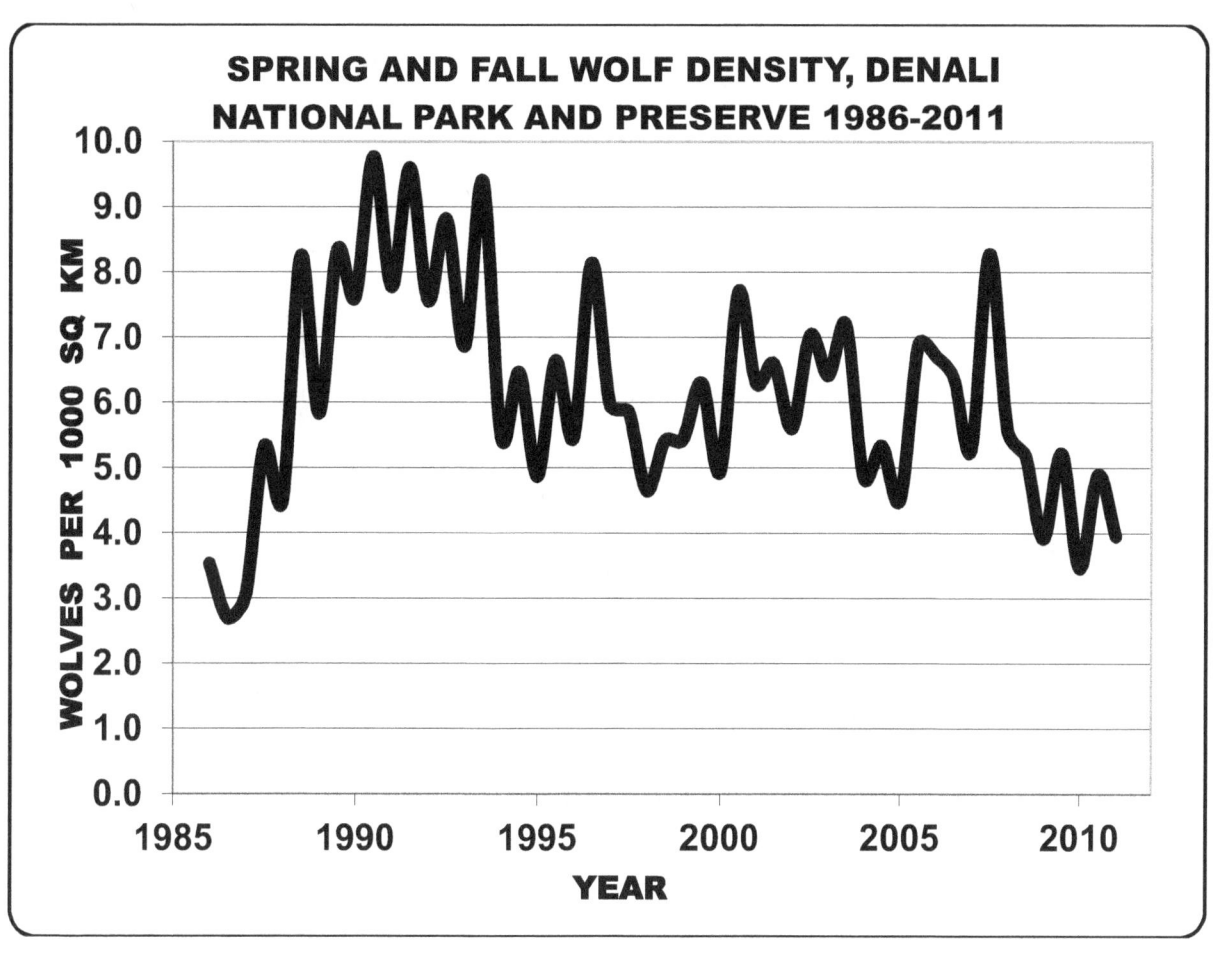

Figure 9. Wolf density estimates, Denali National Park and Preserve, 1986-2011, spring and fall estimates on the same plot.

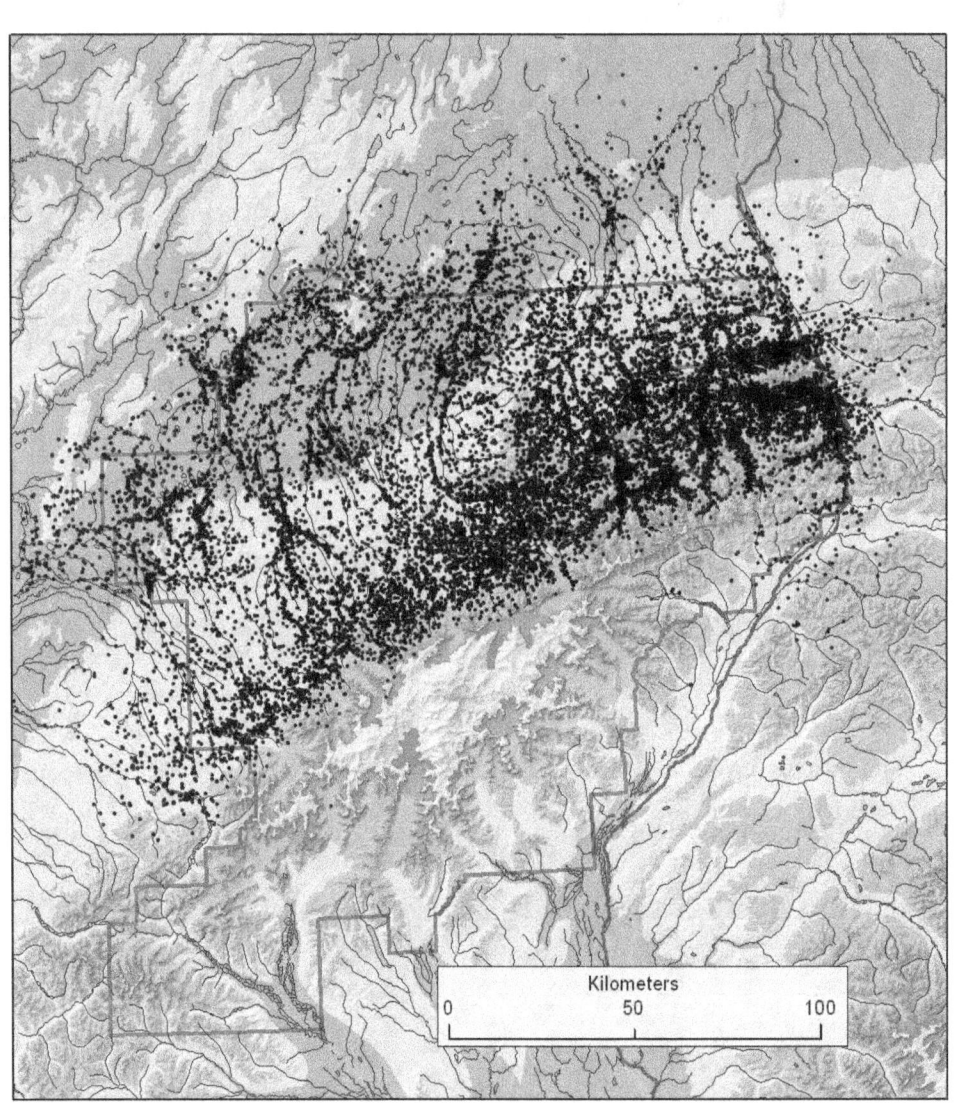

Figure 10. Locations of VHF- and GPS-collared wolves, 1986-2011.

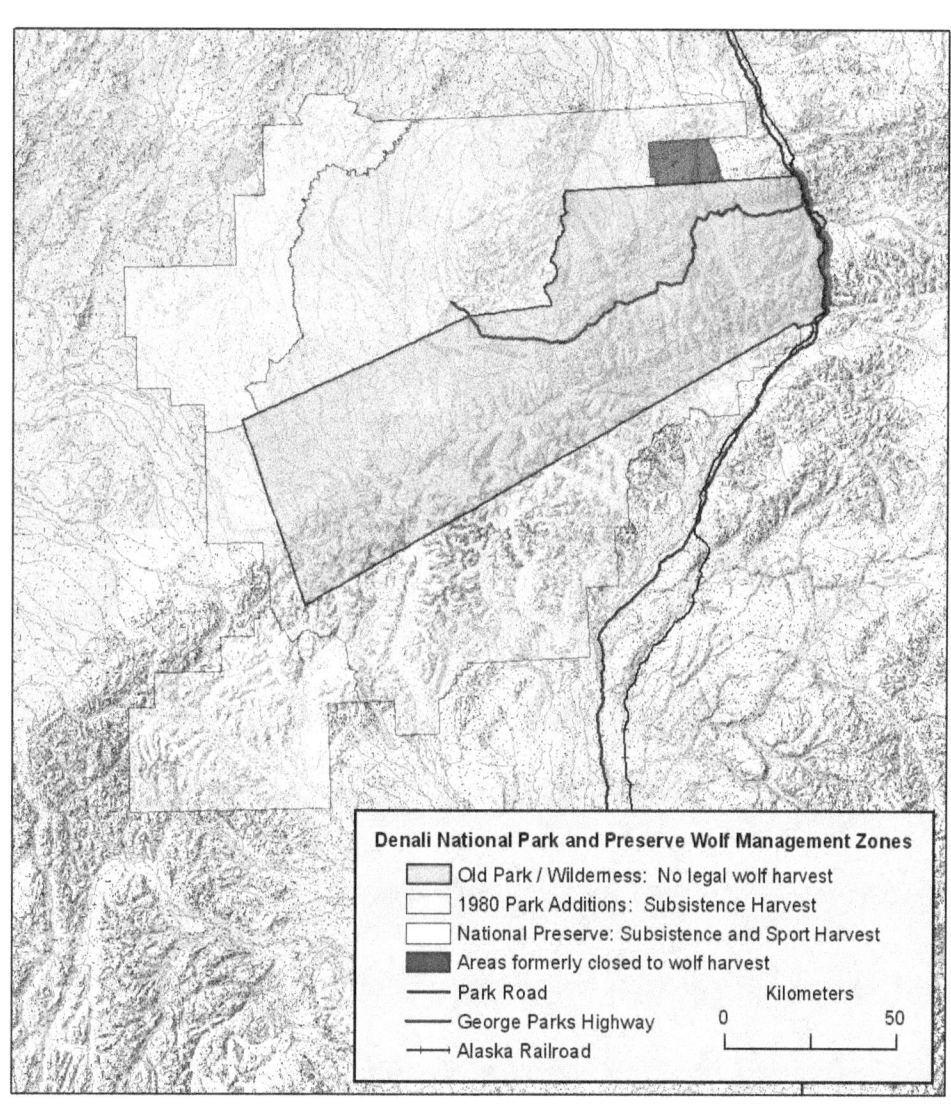

Figure 11. Denali National Park and Preserve, showing areas of differing wolf management.